THE CRITICAL CONNECTIONS

FOR SUCCESS IN EVERY RELATIONSHIP

Leaders. Educators. Employees. Families. Friends. Church.

K. Lynn Wade

ISBN 979-8-89243-141-5 (paperback)
ISBN 979-8-89428-225-1 (hardcover)
ISBN 979-8-89243-142-2 (digital)

Christian Faith Publishing
832 Park Avenue
Meadville, PA 16335
www.christianfaithpublishing.com

Printed in the United States of America

To all the individuals who have contributed to the insights that have revealed the critical connections in relationship development. Also, to my wife, Linda, who has been an encouragement to finish writing this, with the inspiration of our two children, Amy and Jeremy and their families. I thank Peyton Hollis, my granddaughter, for her editing the first draft and for the cover design.

- Understanding the critical connections on relationship building
- Analyzing where you are in a relationship
- Learning how to improve a relationship

—Lynn Wade, MEd.
Leadership consultant and educator

CONTENTS

Introduction: Case Studies ix

Chapter 1:   Setting the Direction 1

Chapter 2:   Heart and Mind 6

Chapter 3:   Leadership Skills.............................10

Chapter 4:   Relationships—Assignment..............14

Chapter 5:   The Critical Connections—
             an Exercise 19

Chapter 6:   Critical Connection Template 23

Chapter 7:   Proctor's Spiral of Futility 38

Chapter 8:   Seeing the Faces.............................50

Chapter 9:   Hope...54

Chapter 10: Strategies to Turn Around a
             Relationship 56

Chapter 11: The Family...................................61

Chapter 12: The Workplace..............................64

Chapter 13: Leadership...................................67

INTRODUCTION

Case Studies

"Leadership is about making others better as a result of your presence, making sure that impact lasts in your absence." Sheryl Sandberg

What follows is the result of years of reflection not only on my relationships but also on those of others who have asked me to help with their relationships. During the years I was assigned the responsibility of training hundreds of school administrators, district administrators, and faculties for the eighth largest school district in America, the critical connections in both relationship formation *and* deterioration became very apparent. Patterns in critical connections became evident to me when I witnessed them over and over. Regardless of a person's position or title, age or sex, critical connections are a constant element in healthy, vibrant relationships.

On the other hand, sadly, the reverse is true and may explain why there are certain broken relationships that result in family violence, school shootings, and other forms of horrors and tragedies.

This book is written to help the readers understand their own relationships with others of any position or title and why coworkers at times do not get along. It is my desire that every reader will become more proactive, proficient, and deliberate in forming, repairing, and building relationships.

The following pages explain how this goal can be accomplished with family and friends, coworkers, employers, and employees. The template laid out in the upcoming chapters applies to all our relationships.

For example, as it was good for me to examine my relationship with one of my new bosses, I then began to evaluate my relationships with those who had formerly reported to me when I was a school principal. I analyzed these relationships to see why I was successful with some and not so successful with others when it came to leadership.

I first observed the principles of critical connections "template" in the workplace and soon came to realize there is a very common and sequential critical connections "template" that is the same in all relationships. This template applies to couples who fall in love and marry and to those who work together in any capacity, from acquaintances to the best of friends.

I have observed this phenomenon in many relationships—from leaders or followers. Hundreds of assistant principals, for instance, have contacted me to help them in their relationships with their principals. Sadly, even though the principal selected the person to be their assistant principal, the relationship deteriorated and needed repair. The damage not only hurt their working relationship, but it had a negative impact on the school.

Many principals contacted me to help them analyze and repair their relationship with employees, students, and the district office. Their situation hurt the school's success and derailed career aspirations.

I have observed the critical connections template in diverse settings across the spectrum—including businesses, education, churches, community groups, and families.

The template I will introduce to you has been used successfully to identify where a relationship is, why it has gotten to that point, and then finally, how to rebuild it. What is interesting is the template's wide application: An employee can use it to reestablish a relationship with a boss, an employer with an employee, or a spouse with the other spouse.

As you read the pages of this book, you will see the faces of those who are loyal to you. However, you will also see those who have undermined you in your personal or professional life. This exercise will be important for you, for in doing so, you will be able to determine where these persons are on the critical connections template with reference to each relationship and how some can be salvaged.

CHAPTER 1

Setting the Direction

> *Connecting is a choice.*
> *Connection always begins with a*
> *commitment to someone else.*
> *People may hear your words, but*
> *they feel your attitude.*
>
> —John Maxwell

Leadership is vital in every organization—whether to a family, a very small business, a nonprofit organization, a PTA, a school, the military, etc. Leadership determines the organization's success in every situation. Organizations do not rise above the identified leader.

As you read this book, you can search through the files of your mind for any setting and identify the individuals you have determined to be exceptional leaders versus those who inflicted serious damage upon the organization.

It is important to match the needs of an organization and the skill set of a leader. I am amazed how frequently a person with very capable skills is appointed to a leadership position, but their skill set is not the one that can essentially move the organization forward. There is a gap between the skillset of the person being hired for the leadership role and the leadership needs for the organization.

I have watched a person be appointed with a great skillset as an instructional leader but lack the skills to develop the culture to nurture unity. You may go to the dentist's office to have your teeth cleaned, but you would not have that same person perform a root canal on you. The same office, the same teeth, yet different needed skillsets for the position. I have seen people who are great at identifying the needed procedures and structure for an institution but who totally lack the people skills to make it happen.

The damage that is done to an organization can be devastating. Coaches are removed, and people in business and education are also replaced when they do not provide the needed leadership for success. Lives can be negatively impacted; reputation, trust, and respect are destroyed. The organization finds itself reaching a breaking point, past any hope of recovery. Relationships and culture are directly affected, in good and bad ways, by every leader.

The most important resource in any organization, regardless of the product or the size, is the people. All are stakeholders, whether we are referring to the employers, the employees, or the clients and customers. The following pages are about turning employees around and having them give you, their leader, their very best.

Certainly, some employees are self-motivated and will always try to give their very best, but others are tempted to leave where they are employed to work elsewhere. It is not uncommon for the boss in that situation to be offended and hold it against the person. A sad fact is that the boss is usually the reason the person leaves the organization. It has been said that people join companies but leave their bosses.

As you read the following pages, you will envision the faces of employees who are costing your organization serious money. Certainly, there is no "silver bullet"—a cure-all that is simple, cheap, and guaranteed to work in turning an employee into a star. I know certain leaders who possess tremendous talent, but they lack the understanding or willingness to implement the steps that would increase the loyalty and work ethic of nearly everyone who works for them. As productive as their workforce is, it could be greater.

There is a first single factor that can be implemented immediately. It will cost you nothing, and as a leader, it comes as close as possible to a "cure-all." This is equally true for parents and appointed leaders in a school, congregation, or business. Many of us grew up hearing the Wheaties cereal slogan, "The Breakfast of Champions." The truth is that leaders do possess the power to find the sleeping champion hidden within nearly every person. There are many

skills and qualities a leader must possess to be successful and effective; however, there is one practice
that research and surveys deem critical.

We can scan our minds' files and see the faces
of engaged, somewhat engaged, and disengaged
employees. I am sure you can think of a few employees who are totally truly engaged. Based on a recent
Gallup study, only one-third are truly engaged, while
18 percent are actively disengaged.

This book has been written after many years
of self-reflection in various leadership roles during
which I listened to and observed hundreds of others
that I have either critiqued or read about. The principle is consistent in all settings. It is my hope that,
as you read the following pages, you will take time to
seriously reflect on your own leadership abilities.

Why are some employees loyal to you and the
success of the organization, but others can't wait
to undermine you? What can you do to encourage
those people to be committed to you and loyal? And
not blind loyalty, but commitment that is based on
important (key) leadership factors. There have been
dictators with tremendous influence; however, I am
not at any time talking about coercion and threats or
power, but genuine leadership.

Before I wrote the following pages, these
thoughts weighed heavily on my heart and mind for
years. I thoroughly studied the guiding principles
in effective leadership and seriously reflected on my
own successes and failures with individuals who have
worked for me—all of which has helped me identify

the *critical connections* consistent with my research on this significant subject. The information you will read has been taught in many venues that I have led. After the training, there have always been those who have expressed to me just how helpful the template on relationship building is, how relationships deteriorate and how to rebuild them. The training has been an eye-opener for them. When they implemented the strategies, they reported their relationships completely changed.

There was a time in history when we heard a lot about "weapons of mass destruction." For those in leadership positions, most have probably known individuals who have been weapons of mass destruction to their organizations. They poison a team or a department and seriously wreak havoc on the reputation, culture, productivity, and careers of others. They might possess the skills needed to do their job, but their attitude is like a cancer to the workplace. Let us identify where they are on our scale in the critical connections template. This will be essential to our task and is the heart of where we are going.

So let's get started.

CHAPTER 2

Heart and Mind

A good head and a good heart are always a formidable combination.

—Nelson Mandela

The principles presented in the following chapters address this key relationship concept—the Heart and Mind. Leadership can be defined as truly seeking to cause others to want your leadership.

In every organization, there are those who clearly understand your expectations, the job requirements, the organizational goals and values, and the rules. However, when observed more closely, there are those who are not committed to diligently following the expectations. It is important to understand that all behavior has a purpose, whether it is appropriate or inappropriate.

So then, why do people ignore the rules when it is obvious they understand them? The same principle applies to you personally. Why do people jaywalk, exceed the speed limit, or violate any simple rule of the law? The reason can be seen by a leader in a workplace when employees ignore the rules, or when parents or teachers are dismayed when their children are not obeying.

We can conclude they do have the rules or regulations in their minds; they just haven't placed them in their hearts. That is the major difference.

The Hebrews 8:10 (KJV) scripture states, "For this is the covenant that I will make with the house of Israel after those days, saith the Lord; I will put my laws into their mind, and write them on their hearts: and I will be to them a God, and they shall be to me a people." What is the difference between having something "in your heart" and having it "in your mind"? The individuals who are loyal and committed to you as a leader have made certain connections with their hearts. For example, what do wives really want, their husband's hearts or minds? If they have their husband's hearts, then they will already have their minds. Possessing a person's heart requires commitment and loyalty. Sadly, some find that they lack their spouse's heart. The consequence may be an easy justification of one's actions, contrary to earlier commitment and loyalty to their entire relationship.

This book is designed to help you understand the formula of critical connections for capturing the hearts of your employees. Many books on leadership tell us that you can lead others with the heart, but you lead yourself with your mind. What is the difference? As a leader, of course, you must be analytical and rational for the organization's best interest. Competence in a variety of skills is essential in leadership, and our mind is the control center for this. Additionally, you must touch the hearts of your followers to influence them to use their hearts to make your organization succeed. Only then will the critical connections flourish.

The goals of the book

1. Get a higher percentage of employees to be fully engaged in their assigned work.
2. Heal broken relationships and strengthen employees' desire to be loyal and committed to both you and the business and organization as a whole.
3. Increase your company's productivity and profit margin.
4. Cut down on the number of employees who decide to leave your organization after money is spent on their development and training.
5. Nurture your business and organization and increase its capacity and effectiveness.

6. Help individuals analyze their personal and professional relationships and seek to make the necessary repairs for valuable and productive relationships.
7. Provide hope.

I can live for two months on a good compliment. (Mark Twain)

You can buy people's time: you can buy their physical presence at a given place; you can even buy a measured number of their muscular motions per hour. But you cannot buy enthusiasm... you cannot buy loyalty...you cannot buy the devotion of their hearts. You must earn these. (Clarence Francis)

CHAPTER 3

Leadership Skills

<blockquote>
One key to successful leadership is continuous personal change. Personal change is a reflection of our inner growth and empowerment.

—Robert E. Quinn
</blockquote>

Being a visionary, understanding how to bring about change, possessing sound decision-making skills, and being organized are just a few of the tools in a much larger bag of critical leadership skills. I would propose, in addition, that understanding and nurturing relationships are the critical connections to a leader's success.

<blockquote>
I will pay more for the ability to handle people than for any other talent under the sun. (John D. Rockefeller)
</blockquote>

Living in Florida, I am very much aware of hurricanes. These storms have been devastating to many areas in our state and neighboring states. As we begin to track a hurricane, and it appears to be heading for Tampa, I begin to think through the "points of vulnerability" of *my own* house in reference to the storm. I keep plywood and two-by-fours, along with other supplies, on hand year-round. In the same way, every leader has points of vulnerability.

We are appointed to positions of leadership—not "anointed," and all of our shortcomings do not just disappear by sunrise on the first day on the job. After we are appointed to a leadership position, it is essential that we develop plans to transform our points of vulnerability into strengths. We may work many years without our points of vulnerability being tested. Sadly, many leaders have derailed when those areas unexpectedly come under fire. A person may get comfortable with the routine and feel they have had some success and begin to coast. This is not leadership.

I had a leader who never let any of us get comfortable in our position. Rather than allowing both of our feet in the comfort zone, she was observant and skilled to make certain we had one foot in a growth zone. Both feet out of the comfort zone constantly will cause serious stress. Knowing the balance is critical—Not only for those the person leads but for the leader. It is absolutely essential for anyone in leadership to prevent catching the "destination disease" and simply coasting. This can happen when a leader reaches certain goals in a position and stops growing.

When a person is appointed to a leadership position, it is only an initial statement that someone believes the right person for the job is now in that role. It is then up to that person to lead in such a way to validate that the correct decision has been made and to keep growing. Sadly, this is not always the case.

It is wise for every person in a leadership position to be honest regarding their skills, knowledge, and developmental needs. True leaders will astutely address each of these qualities just as vigorously as they would expect from a person further down the ladder as an employee.

With this in mind, we now focus on relationship development. We will now consider those who are eager to grow professionally, those who are fragile or deteriorating, and those who are ready to "go postal" with inappropriate behavior, and we will consider the keys a leader can use in turning them in the direction of success.

During my time in college, I am amazed that we were never offered a course on relationships. This was true during my time as a student earning my bachelor's and graduate degrees. The required course, Foundations of Education did not address it. As a teacher and then an administrator, I was never offered a workshop on relationships. I have come to know relationships are at the heart of instruction, and relationships are at the heart of leadership. A teacher may be a master at developing lessons that best teach a needed skill, but if the relationship with the students is lacking, it is all for naught. It falls on deaf ears. A principal may understand budgets, schedules, strategic planning, but still not understand relationship building and culture, sadly, the organization will never be or have all it is capable of accomplishing. Relationships are at the heart of the family, the congregation, any business, school, corporation, or government entity.

For example, seeking a degree in Business or a degree in Biblical Studies for those who desire to be an evangelist, a course in relationships is missing; and in Business it is all about connecting with people. An evangelist studies the Bible and reads on every page about relationships. When they are seeking to bring people to Christ, again it is about relationships. I would submit that prior to a person serving in Congress, there should be a prerequisite course on relationships. Whether in Education, Law, or in Medicine, a course should include the importance of strict relationships.

By completing the following exercises, you will lay the foundation you need for studying your employees, which we will cover in the rest of the book.

We lead by being human. We do not lead by being corporate, by being professional, or by being institutional. (Paul Hawken, founder, Smith & Hawken)

CHAPTER 4

Relationships—Assignment

*The most important single ingredient
in the formula of success is knowing
how to get along with people.*

—Theodore Roosevelt

I. Workplace employee analysis

    A. Identify *one to three* employees who are your strongest, most loyal allies. These are the persons who are highly motivated to support you through thick or thin.

       Please write down their names:

       1. __________________________

       2. __________________________

       3. __________________________

B. Now, who are *one to three* persons at work who you consider to be adversarial? The persons who work against you behind your back, do not give you the benefit of the doubt, and will undermine any initiative you try to implement.

Please write down their names.

1. _______________________________
2. _______________________________
3. _______________________________

C. What do your *loyal* employees have in common with you?

Please list the commonalities.

1. _______________________________
2. _______________________________
3. _______________________________
4. _______________________________
5. _______________________________

D. What do the *disloyal* employees on your list have in common with you?

Please list the commonalities.

1. _______________________________
2. _______________________________

3. ______________________________
4. ______________________________
5. ______________________________

E. Next, write down the names of the *five top influencers* at your work site. This is not based on the title but rather their level of influence.

1. ______________________________
2. ______________________________
3. ______________________________
4. ______________________________
5. ______________________________

Note: It is important for us to reflect and identify individuals as we move through the step-by-step process of relationship analysis. We will eventually analyze your relationship with key influencers. Every person who has a positive impact on the workplace or those who feign their support, either way, affect the work ethic and attitude of others. Those who are working against the accomplishment of the vision are undermining the culture and values of the organization. Human relationship capacity building in every organization is essential for reaching its potential.

II. Relationships outside of the workplace

A. Identify *one to three* individuals in another setting who are your strongest allies and loyal partners. These are the persons who are highly motivated to support you through thick or thin.

Please write down their names:

1. _______________________________
2. _______________________________
3. _______________________________

B. Now, who are *one to three* individuals who work against you behind your back, do not give you the benefit of the doubt, and will undermine any initiative you try to implement.

Please write down these persons' names.

1. _______________________________
2. _______________________________
3. _______________________________

C. What do these *loyal* individuals have in common with you?

Please list the commonalities.

1. _______________________________
2. _______________________________
3. _______________________________
4. _______________________________
5. _______________________________

Note: It is important to reflect on our personal relationships. Those within our family, our neighbors, and all other social groups. The critical connections for success apply to all relationships. The exercise will help analyze where we are with those in our circle.

The next activity requires you to give serious thought to the nature of relationships—the critical connections. We will be considering how they develop and why they come unraveled.

CHAPTER 5

The Critical Connections— an Exercise

> *I've learned that people will forget what you said, people will forget what you did, but people will never forget how you made them feel.*
>
> —Maya Angelou

Please give thought to the seven words I have listed below and consider their definitions.

Commitment—Pledge, promise.
Trust—Firm belief in the honesty, trustworthiness, power of a person, being relied upon
Appreciation—To think highly of, approval

Loyalty—Consistently true and faithful
Empowerment—To enable, to give power or authority
Respect—High regard, esteem
Ownership—Right of possession, mutual stock and investment

In any relationship, whether personal or professional, is there a set of sequential steps of development? Does one of the seven words always appear first in the sequence, with a specific one following, and so on? Or have you come to the conclusion that there is no set pattern? Do you believe the pattern varies; if so, how?

It is extremely beneficial for you to complete the following exercise to the best of what you believe is the pattern. On the critical connections chart to be completed, there are seven lines. Line seven is the last step. Please take the seven words and place them in a sequence of step number 1, and progress to the highest level in a relationship, step number 7. Place the seven words in the sequence that you believe they develop in a relationship. The relationship can be with a person you report to, or a person who reports to you. It might also be a spouse, your child, a friend, a coworker, and the like.

The *Critical Connections* for Success
in Every Relationship

1.

2.

3.

4.

5.

6.

7.

Commitment
Trust
Appreciation
Loyalty
Empowerment
Respect
Ownership

Do you believe your sequence is true in all or most relationships?

Do you believe that the stages of development in your personal relationships are the same as those in your professional relationships?

I strongly believe there is a pattern in the developmental stages of all relationships. Understanding them allows us to identify where we are in our relationships and how others view us.

Frequently in relationships, individuals may be at the same stage of development with one another. It does not always play out that way, but it happens quite often. Not only will we specifically identify what step of relationship development we are on with another individual, but we will also identify strategies on how you can further develop relationships with your boss, employees, coworkers, spouse, friends, and so forth.

In the next chapter, I will provide you with what I believe is the consistent sequence of *critical connections*—the qualities in relationship development, whether personal or professional.

It is not essential for us to agree 100% with the sequence of the steps in a relationship. It is more important to work through the exercise and give serious thought and reflection on relationship development.

CHAPTER 6

Critical Connection Template

> *The essence of leadership is relationship;*
> *influencing people to achieve things*
> *together that can't be achieved alone.*
>
> —Leonard Sweet

The normal order—the critical connections—of relationship development is **appreciation**, followed by *respect*, then *trust*, and then *empowerment*. Following empowerment is *commitment*, then *ownership*, and finally *loyalty*.

Appreciation is the foundation of every healthy relationship. It is the cornerstone of relationships. If one does not feel appreciated, it is difficult for any relationship to be developed any further.

Please consider the following rationale for the sequence of the critical connections in relationship development. First, we can appreciate a person and never meet them or never really get to know them. You can call a business, and the person you are speaking with goes out of his or her way to help you. This is your first encounter with that person. At this point, you do not know enough about the individual to respect him, but you do know you appreciate what he has done for you.

There was a time when I needed supplies for the school where I was principal. The problem I encountered was that it was not the day of the week when we were allowed to make emergency pickups for supplies. I called the warehouse for needed school supplies, and a lady answered, whom I had never met or spoken to prior to that occasion.

I pleaded my case to her, and she made an exception and allowed me to go to the warehouse. When I arrived at the warehouse, I did not see the lady who had helped me on the phone, so I sent her a card to thank her for her help and to express my appreciation.

A couple of days passed, and she called me. She wanted to personally thank me for the card. She said it was the first time anyone had expressed appreciation for anything she had done at work. As a result, she told me I did not have to worry about what day of the week I would be permitted to pick up supplies at the warehouse. I was just to call her, and she would have the order pulled and waiting for me on the loading dock. Did I appreciate her? Certainly! We had never met, nor did I really know anything about her, but she had taken the time to help me out when I found my school in a bind.

The expression of appreciation is processed through the mind and does something very special. It penetrates the heart. That which penetrates the heart can change a person's self-image, attitude, and commitment. As the Wheaties cereal box once claimed to be the "Breakfast of Champions," appreciation is the stimulant that can change an employee's commitment. Validation and affirmation are given through appreciation.

Many principals who have attended the training on critical connections and put in place the key principles of touching the heart have stated the employee who gave them the greatest trouble became their strongest advocate. I have seen this turn around marriages, parent-child relationships, teacher-student relationships, and the like. This is truly a game changer that costs nothing but is worth gold.

When you ask someone how to soften and reach a person's heart and not just their mind, it appears to be a question few people have considered. You can touch the heart every time you take a deliberate action to increase a person's self-esteem, respond with empathy and compassion, seek to help and encourage, listen rather than dictate, and provide active support. The heart may have become hardened, and you will be surprised how long and what action it will take to begin to soften the heart for them to be receptive. Don't give up, you do not know how long it will take to soften the heart. If you do not make the breakthrough, you will know you have truly tried as a leader.

I would next ask, with reference to *respect and trust*, "Who would you tell a secret to, someone you respect or someone you trust?" People usually answer, "The person I trust." I would agree. Trust is a higher level in a relationship than respect. Respect is to hold someone in high regard. I may respect something about a person but not necessarily trust him.

I have known people I deeply respected due to their skillfulness in an area that was important causing me to hold their expertise in high regard. Competence and character must both be present for trust to take place—if either one of these diminish, trust will be destroyed. A person might have impeccable character but be greatly lacking in competence and therefore excessive in poor decision-making. For this reason, there would be a lack of trust. The opposite scenario is also true: A person may be highly skilled and possess admired leadership skills that set a person apart from other leaders, but the person may have a flawed character. For example, he may give different answers to various individuals, and when employees compare notes, they realize the boss does not tell the truth. He is considered a liar, and trust is then destroyed. It is clear that for trust to exist, competence and character must both be present.

Trust becomes an important factor in any political race. When it is election season, you can be confident opposing political parties will push a trust factor against the opposing candidate. Whether for local positions or national offices. They will either attack the person's character or their competence. The goal is to destroy trust in the opposing candidate.

Trust is also developed on an individual basis with each employee individually. Frequently, bosses feel the pain of frustration when they have worked very hard and feel they have made decisions that benefit the employees. Then they wonder, "After all I have done, why don't they give me the benefit of the doubt and trust me? Unbelievable!" *The benefit of the doubt is the dividend of Trust earned.*

I've observed that leaders misunderstand how trust is *earned*. It is earned by one employee at a time. The same course of action might affect three employees. It reflects the leader's competence, character, and appreciation. Two individuals may extend their trust, while the third could still consider "the verdict is out" based on previous experiences with this particular boss (or a previous boss).

The employee wants to be certain, so more evidence or proof must be exhibited before the person crosses the line to say the boss has earned his trust. Something the boss did in the past places a major warning sign in the mind of that particular employee, and he/she has not determined the boss worthy of trust. Once trust is destroyed, it takes a long time hopefully to restore.

I have seen bosses go to great lengths to provide breakfasts or lunches for their employees and many other expressions of appreciation. Frequently, events such as these are only internalized on an individual basis and are received as mere tokens of appreciation. Leaders then conclude they have *earned* the trust. Rather than *earn*, they really believe they have merited the trust. When people believe they have merited or earned trust by what they have done, they themselves do not realize they do not determine when trust takes place.

This is a major mistake in our thinking that takes place too often with leaders, between friends, married couples, and the like. Events, actions, decisions, and all behaviors of the leader are individually internalized and weighed, and then the person determines if enough has been done to merit his or her trust in the competence and character of the leader. Giving gifts or tokens of appreciation may cause the receiver to feel an obligation, but this does not earn trust.

I have seen faculties divided by numerous school administrators whose schools received money from the state for meritorious test scores. The administrators, with the best of intentions, developed various formulas for which employees receive financial compensation because students took the tests, and employees were responsible for the outstanding test scores. The employees who received the thousands of dollars did not increase in trust because of such a gift. There were times when they saw the lack of competence in the decision of the distribution of the funds and thought less of the administrator.

Trust was broken and a schoolwide division over money was the result.

I know employees who have no idea where they stand with their boss. But discussions with their various bosses reveal that they are confident; they express their appreciation for and significantly value their employees. Therefore, it is evident that employees have a need for something that singles them out personally or publicly. I have seen this run the course more times than I can count. Bosses are adamant regarding their appreciation, and employees are just as adamant about the lack of appreciation shown.

So let's go back to our critical connections template. The first step is *appreciation*, the second step is *respect*, and the third step is *trust*.

For any leader to be effective, trust is a prerequisite. A leader might have his eye on the bottom line and exert extreme pressure for great performance, but he may only get the bare minimum performance. Appreciation, respect, and trust have not been nurtured intentionally or properly, and, as a result, minimum effort is all the leader receives.

A worker can arrive at work, get coffee, check personal emails, get another coffee, and then think, "Since it's close to breaking time, why get started?" By lunchtime, maybe half an hour of work takes place between personal phone calls, Internet searches, and the like. After lunch, the worker has time to visit with coworkers, drink more coffee, make personal phone calls, check the Internet, and possibly play Solitaire on the computer. Basically, the person is involved in task avoidance with no commitment to the leader or the company.

Employees are the most important resource to any organization. Leaders who do not see the need for appreciation and instead believe that salaries and benefits are the primary solution do not understand what motivates the majority of employees. A strong boss does not always equate to effective or inspiring leadership.

Appreciation is not only the initial step in relationship development, but it is seriously desired by employees.

> [Forty-six percent] 46% of those who quit their jobs last year did so because they felt unappreciated. Another 65% of respondents said they would work harder if they felt like their contributions would be noticed by management. (US Department of Labor)

Step number 4 is *empowerment*, followed by *commitment*, then *ownership*, and last, *loyalty*. I am not as locked into the order of the last four. I admit this order is simply my opinion. What is critical, however, is that you understand, analyze, and study these four steps and understand how relationship connections develop and how they are violated and destroyed.

As a freshman in college, there was a certain class where I intentionally sat in the back of the room. When the lecture got boring, I would cautiously shift my focus of attention to a female student named Linda, who sat a few rows in front of me. She was very attractive, intelligent, and friendly. For months, I admired her at a distance. We had no interactions, but I did *appreciate* her. I appreciated the way she cared for herself and the kindness she showed to those around her. I eventually built the courage to ask her out on a date. As I got to know her, I held her in high regard for her values. (Or you could say it another way: I *respected* her.) As we continued to date, we shared many things in conversation, which included secrets. Obviously, we had earned each other's *trust* to do this. Frequently, she would want to go out on Friday and had mentioned where she would like to go on a date. Both of us would make such decisions or provide input on where and what we wanted to do on dates. This was the fourth step in the relationship, known as *empowerment*. Empowerment is to enable another individual to make decisions that will be of benefit for the whole. Those individuals who merit trust in an organization or any relationship have earned the right to make decisions that will be of benefit to the couple or organization. After all, they are the most important resource in the partnership. They bring their own unique perspective that contributes to an amazing synergy. Empowerment contributes to their buy-in. Ultimately, we made a commitment, followed by ownership or oneness, being in it together, which involves loyalty.

To make a commitment is to promise, buy in, and support. When a person is empowered, they have an investment in the organization and therefore *commitment* follows. When a person buys in with commitment, there is a oneness or *ownership*. They have skin in the game. The person is committed, devoted, and attached. Simply put, they have *loyalty* to the other party or organization. In time, we walked down the aisle and made our vows to each other. Ultimately, we made a *commitment*, and with that, followed *ownership* or *oneness*, and then *loyalty*.

The same sequence of developmental relationship steps took place after Linda and I married and looked for a contractor to build us a house. We identified three builders whose work we *appreciated*. As we continued to research the builders, we gained *respect* and *trust* for them. There was one who stood out from the rest, and serious discussions followed. We were *empowered* to pick the colors, carpets, light fixtures, and other items we desired. Linda and I agreed to the terms of *empowerment* the builder would possess, such as the choice of subcontractors and the like. We then signed a contract and made the *commitment*. Once the contract was signed, both parties understood the project's *ownership* terms and the *loyalty* to the contract both parties were to uphold.

Let us critique the critical connections we have covered and place them against any relationship. I believe in your personal, social and professional relationships, you will see the consistent pattern of the development of the steps.

The sequence of developmental steps is very important in understanding and repairing relationships. Two people, whether in a personal or professional relationship, may reach the critical connection of loyalty. We all know that without work, loyalty will not stay at that level. It might begin to unravel, and once it drops below trust it will take much more than an apology to restore the relationship to vibrancy. An apology can help with the correction, but it does not remove the natural consequence of the caution that now exists in the relationship. A person may get upset when, after his or her apology, even if accepted, did not restore the relationship to what it once enjoyed. If trust is injured, an apology does not remove the damage or the consequences. "Divorces" do take place not only between husbands and wives but also between employees and employers, between neighbors, between teachers and students, between coworkers, and between individuals in various settings.

Once any relationship reaches this point, it will not accomplish the purpose or vision intended. Often, various paybacks or sabotage behaviors will take place. This attitude not only destroys the intended relationship but impacts everyone around them. Whether it is a student and a teacher, a teacher and an administrator, a husband and wife, a parent and child, those around them are pulled in to take sides and everyone loses.

It is easy to argue that employees are hired to do a job and receive a salary that is agreed upon, and ultimately, it is up to them to perform accordingly. The flip side of the argument is that a leader is to take the lead—certainly as a change agent and a visionary who is in touch with what will provide the greatest dividends for the organization. It would naturally follow that as a visionary, the leader would be able to see what the current output of every direct report is and to determine what that employee is really capable of doing. Organizational effectiveness weighs in the balance of all relationships and capacity building. A leader should be the catalyst for change, and this principle requires a leader to take the actions necessary to bring out the best in all employees.

All of us continue to return to a restaurant, grocery store, business, and the like because of the special treatment we were shown as customers. Appreciation, kindness, gratitude, and respect are clearly evident to us. We have also experienced situations where there is a breakdown in appreciation, and loyalty never occurs. Perhaps we did not return to a business because of the poor treatment we received from the employees. When we feel disrespected or just in their way, we do not return, no matter how good the quality of the product. Employees who don't seem to care may reflect their boss's lack of care.

You were asked earlier to make several lists of names and commonalities. Consider the list of names of people you identified who you consider extremely loyal to you. I suspect you can see the commonalities among them. They are individuals who feel appreciated by you. Their respect and trust for you have been earned. You have empowered them because you trust them. You are committed to them, and you have touched their hearts. Therefore, they seek to be a viable contributor with a sense of pride in ownership, tackling various projects and responsibilities. You have appreciated and affirmed them and the value of their work. You have built a very strong bridge that connects to them. You have captured their hearts, not just their minds. They will do whatever needs to be done for the sake of the organization. Extra hours and additional responsibilities are eagerly given. It is their thanks to you—their gratitude for you.

Now consider your other list. Those who do not want to be there and are out as soon as they can possibly leave will do nothing extra to help the organization and spread organizational cancer to whoever will listen to them. Certainly, they are not loyal or committed. You don't trust them, and they don't trust you. The bottom line is that they do not feel appreciated, and their relationship with the boss is strained.

Similarly, divorced husbands and wives take up separate living quarters and move on. Employees do that at times, but they remain with the organization very often, and all those who encounter them are affected by their attitude. They choose not to move on and hope you will. It is up to the leader to take the first step. The leader must take the lead to either rebuild the relationship or help the person understand the need to consider a change professionally.

The leader has the responsibility to say or do something that will benefit the development of the employee. Quoting from *A Love Worth Living*, "If you had food and saw a person starving, would you not share it? If you had water and saw a person dying of thirst, would you not give it?" Of course, you would. Then won't you do the same for the hearts of those who work for you? Your employees thirst for your approval and appreciation.

When the heart may have hardened, you will need to be patient with how long it takes to soften. The heart did not get that way overnight, and one simple statement of appreciation or asking for forgiveness most likely will not be enough. I worked in a hospital for a couple of years in respiratory therapy. Our team would respond when they would announce a Code Blue or a Code 19. The standard procedure was for the doctor to shock the heart to get it to begin beating again. Frequently we waited as the doctor would need to try and try again. It is very much like the need for appreciation and the possible need for repeating the actions that touch the heart.

There was a certain position I was appointed to during my career in education, but the person who was to be over me had someone else in mind for the position. Those in higher positions determined I was the person for the job. For several months, I was very limited in responsibilities due to my supervisor not being happy with my selection. I had to put my feelings aside and simply keep on keeping on and move forward. I began showing sincere appreciation to my new boss. The appreciation began to soften my boss's heart. As time passed, I was asked by my boss to fill in at meetings to represent our team and to fill in when the boss was out of the office. My relationship with my superior began to change, simply due to continued honest appreciation. Our relationship ascended through the scale of the critical connections to the point of loyalty.

From the time I was a young boy, I often heard the phrase, "Do not back a rattlesnake into a corner!" It is very obvious why. The snake has only one way out when it feels threatened. That places the snake in a very threatened situation, and it is going to come out one way, and it strikes at what it sees as a threat. So I ask, "When does a person feel rejected?" This is a very serious question in understanding relationships, and I suggest the ultimate answer is that people feel *rejected* when they do not feel *appreciated*.

Please stop and reflect before you read the next chapter. Take the seven steps we just covered and put them to the test. Think of positive relationships you enjoy and identify what step you are on with each person. How did you get there? Do you now see how the relationships traveled through the steps to get to loyalty?

CHAPTER 7

Proctor's Spiral of Futility

*Our greatest joy and our greatest pain
come in our relationships with others.*

—Stephen R. Covey

*I don't know why they call it heart break. It feels
like every other part of my body is broken too.*

—Terri Guillemets

While at Rutgers University, Dr. Samuel Proctor had a very enlightening work that connects perfectly with what we have covered thus far. Dr. Proctor points out seven words, each representative of one of the seven sequential stages in the deterioration of relationships. Dr. Proctor stated that the sequence is locked in and that people cannot skip steps.

Over the years, there have been numerous school shootings and other such acts of violence in society. It is my opinion that Dr. Proctor's spiral of futility provides the answer for many of the acts of violence.

All of us find ourselves in many relationships. We experience them at a very personal level within our families. But they also extend into our neighborhood and continue at workplaces, religious congregations, clubs, teams, and so on. In any of these settings, we may find ourselves on Proctor's spiral of futility or be able to identify others on the spiral.

Dr. Proctor made his application to students. My experience, however, is that the steps Dr. Proctor has identified are true in relationships of all people, both children and adults.

Certainly, at any level of leadership, it will be to one's advantage to understand and give serious thought to Dr. Proctor's work. Without question, it will provide a wealth of insight. And perhaps, those in leadership may also find themselves on one of the steps of Dr. Proctor's *spiral of futility.*

We have all observed a person who begins to freefall when a relationship begins to unravel. It goes from bad to worse to total destruction. Leaders need to understand that they have the influence to turn a person around when they begin to tailspin into futility.

Workers, followers, or employees are a leader's most important resource. An individual who is totally loyal to the leader—who has bought into the vision and whose passion is ignited—will expand every ounce of energy in support of the leader and the initiative.

On the other hand, a person who enters the downward spiral will become verbal and hostile and most likely be a cancer to the leader and the organization. Such a person becomes a weapon of mass destruction because of their malignant attitude, verbal assaults, and negativity. Putting a great deal of time and investment into an employee should motivate a leader to key into the spiral, understand the employee, and seek ways to properly reengage and help the person. If the person crashes and burns in a relationship, it will infect other employees' productivity and impede the critical synergy the leader is seeking to achieve.

There is greater success for a leader who reaches out and helps an employee lift a crashing attitude and reach for a new altitude. One in which each muscle is put to work to benefit the organization's goals and mission. The payoff is that the heart and mind are given to the vision of the leader.

Over the years, I have been very fortunate to work with hundreds of people in leadership positions, and I have consistently observed this to be the case. I have used Dr. Proctor's steps on the *spiral of futility* as a template for identification and have the appointed leaders implement strategies to help the person take control of their downward spiral and begin to climb upward. Sometimes, however, the conclusion must be reached that the relationship is indeed bankrupt, and the improbable solution is that one must cut the losses.

In Dr. Proctor's spiral of futility, he points out that step number 1 of the downward spiral is *rejection*. Feelings of rejection follow when appreciation and affirmation are lacking/absent/nonexistent.

When a person does not feel appreciated, they feel their value is minimized and rejection begins to grow. It may be a statement or action that destroys the feeling of being appreciated.

However, feelings do not always equal facts, so feelings of rejection may be falsely perceived as true or false. What feels like rejection by friends, a spouse, or authority still feels real and hurts.

A person can enter the dark cloud of rejection when a promotion does not take place or when there is no explanation of why the person was not promoted. It can be the feeling of nonacceptance for a variety of reasons. It may be values, fashion, cliques, humor, assignments, derogatory comments, preferences, perceived prejudices, being left out, not invited or included in various social get-togethers, and the list continues. More often than not, one honest, deliberate, kind, caring, and compassionate meeting with the individual to clear the air is a step in the right direction. But sadly, way too often, being proactive is ignored, not seen as that important, dismissed, or missed altogether. Then the spiral moves on to the next downward step.

I am confident that as you read these pages, you can identify a time when you felt rejected. It is possible that it did not go any further. Possibly, you placed no value on the one who was rejecting you. Maybe something or someone intervened, and you came off the spiral.

Rejection is followed by the second step of the downward spiral: isolation—whether voluntary or not. What once felt like a comfortable, safe relationship dissipates. Relationship avoidance grows, and the distance begins to widen. This intentional isolation removes the rejected from the rejector but does not help the situation. Rather, it only intensifies the unknown and makes it worse.

Once a person feels rejected, the previously comfortable feeling of a relationship is now gone. The person now begins relationship avoidance, and the distance begins to widen. The person's intentional isolation is an attempt to remove himself from the pain of the relationship. The person begins to question everything and puts the worst possible slant on everything about the relationship. There is minimum interaction and, as a result, less time and occasion to correct the downward spiral.

I suspect we have all seen individuals who have pulled away from another person or group. Maybe we have experienced it ourselves. The individual intends to distance oneself from the pain of rejection. Individuals who feel rejected may very well go to great lengths to do all they can to avoid contact with people who give off the perception of rejection. This is never the remedy and only intensifies the problem.

The second step in the spiral is *isolation*. Isolation is the intentional act from the one causing the pain. If the person is forced to be in the presence of the source of pain, then the person emotionally withdraws. Think of a marriage where there is separation and not a divorce, where an individual is seeking to escape and distance from the relationship.

One child may look at the family dynamics and draw the conclusion that a parent prefers siblings, feels rejected, and then begin to isolate from the family. It may be caused by discipline that is extreme or inappropriate.

When you consider the workplace, you probably can identify a fellow employee who is on this step. They feel rejected and are pulling away from the group.

The third step in the downward spiral is *insulation*. This is a deeper withdrawal intended to insulate the person from pain and hurt. The person is now drifting further from the work group, the institutionalized beliefs, and the values of the organization. In a family, the person is now questioning family values and beliefs. They remove themselves from any family get together and activities. They feel totally justified for becoming their own separate entity. Feeling that nobody cares, serious resentment is building, hope is dying, the emotional pain is severe, and despair grows.

I live in Florida and have worked with many schools. August is the first month of school and the hottest month of the year in Florida. It is not uncommon to see students arriving at school in 96-degree weather with a heavy winter coat and the hood over their head. Why a thick cold-weather coat in August? By knowing many of the students from the previous school year, I recognize they ended the school year feeling rejected. School was painful. They felt like outsiders and believed they did not fit into the system. These students were insulating themselves in August, not from the weather, but from the rejection.

As we work through the steps of Proctor's spiral of futility, can you think back to a time when you found yourself on any of these steps? Or are you there now? In some areas of life, most of us have felt the building of resentment and the escalating feeling of being wronged.

The next and fourth step of Proctor's downward spiral is *hostility*. By this point of rejection, pain has become so all-consuming that hostility is the natural next step. The person has become disagreeable and irritable, ready to verbally spar and ripe to explode. They have become seriously affected by the hurt and are always ready to retaliate verbally and take on anyone. It becomes their mindset; it now controls their thinking, their attitude, and their disposition. It motivates them to be hostile.

This hostile person can be a child in a family reacting toward the rest of the family or the deterioration of the relationship between the parents. It can be a student in school or an employee of the school. It can be a person in any relationship. This person is emotionally charged and verbally and emotionally volatile.

Hostility would be bad enough if it was the final step in the downward spiral. But sadly, there are a few more steps. The fifth step is the *withdrawal of success symbols.* Because this person feels pushed to the outside, they reject anyone being praised or experiencing any kind of success/acknowledgment. There is great resentment toward anyone who adheres to the organizational value system. The person will openly defy a superior or outright refuse to comply. They have reached total justification for not only their withdrawal but also their disruptive and noncooperative attitude. The values, goals, objectives, and individuals who make up the organization are rejected.

The sixth step in Proctor's downward spiral is the *acceptance of failure.* This is a basic message of, "Yes, I will live up to your lowest expectations of me." "I will show you what failure looks like." The person will live it out in all his or her thinking and actions. "You have hurt me, and now I will hurt you and possibly even those you care for."

Each downward step may seem as though there is no reason or hope to move in the opposite, upward direction. It is critical to understand key strategies implemented on any of the steps that will begin to turn around the person's mindset.

The seventh and last step of the downward spiral is *crime and violence.* This involves the intentional lashing out toward those who have catalyzed this person's problems, frustrations, anger, and pain. These individuals feel like they have been dealt a bad hand; since it is unfair, someone should pay. They harbor a need for self-justification and find relief in lashing out and punishing others, even those not involved.

The relationship issues explain the spiral downward to crime and violence. In my fifty-one years of experience, I have witnessed, participated in, and worked with hundreds of principals, assistant principals, students and teachers. As a close observer, I have also witnessed numerous steps of the spiral taking place. I am not a psychologist, doctor, or law enforcement expert, but I am very thankful that only a couple of the relationships I observed led to crime and violence.

I have been asked by married couples, teachers, assistant principals, district administrators, and department heads for help when the relationships go sour. Most of the time, we can identify the stage of the relationship and its current state on the scale. Then we implement strategies to save it. Sadly, in some cases, the relationships are already bankrupt, and nothing can be done to salvage it.

At the conclusion of presenting a training based upon the material in this book, one of the participants who was an assistant principal submitted the following note to me: "Talk about a revelation --looking at the appreciation scale and Proctors spiral of futility,

I have realized that I am on the first two steps of the spiral of feeling rejected and voluntary isolation with respect to my principal. I freely give commitment and trust to those I work for, which is a mistake when someone betrays you; then you lose so much of what is necessary to find joy in your work. Even though five years have gone by, I cannot regain respect and trust for this individual. Dignity and hope? Not at this site. The staff appreciate, respect, trust, and keep me going and I avoid burn-out – or do I?

"I catch glimpses of motivation and inspiration when I attend training and I wonder where the person went? I don't like where I am. I used to write grants, initiate programs, etc. I used to feel up and coming and now I feel old, tired, and used up."

When I read this, it broke my heart. This administrator analyzed for the first time what was happening to the relationship he once had with the principal. He was hurting and withdrawing. He admitted his relationship with the faculty was his saving grace. He was not old, but he was worn out. His relationship with his principal drained his energy, desire, commitment, and hope. I contacted this administrator and worked to help him to come and be all he dreamed of being in his profession. Remember, you can take the initiative to repair the relationship of anyone in your personal or professional life. Determining to make a reconciliation attempt by using sincere appreciation and seeking to soften the heart will hopefully be the beginning of restoring the relationship.

Dr. Proctor emphasized a person descends the steps of the spiral in a sequential order. That person can or will also come out of the spiral step by step. How long a person is on any one step varies. You cannot force a person to improve on the spiral, but you can certainly push them down on the scale.

Dr. Proctor's work is a masterpiece in understanding the steps in dissolving a relationship and the potential damage.

The chart on the following page provides a visual graphic—a template of Proctor's spiral of futility.

Proctor's Spiral of Futility

1. *Rejection*
2. *Isolation*
3. *Insulation*
4. *Hostility*
5. *Withdrawal from success symbols*
6. *Acceptance of Failure*
7. *Crime and Violence*

Dr. Proctor's work, in my estimation, is a *template* that has a very broad application. When I first came across his work in various books written by Robert DeBruyn, the application was identifying students and their relationships in school.

As you reflect on individuals whom you have heard on the news have acted violently, I suggest that, in many cases, they are on step number 7 in Dr. Proctor's work. I believe it can be applied to what took place at Columbine school and other occasions over and over again, not only in schools but also daily in the workplace. Therefore, it is worthy of our consideration.

Don't belittle. Don't put people down. Don't make anyone feel small. Don't be judgmental or critical in ways that diminish another person's sense of themselves. If everyone would live by that principle, you would see most of the problems that we associate with mental health problems disappear. Most of the problems of crime and abuse, academic failures, problems between bosses and workers, broken homes and addictions can be traced to low self-esteem. (Jack Canfield and Jacqueline Miller)

CHAPTER 8

Seeing the Faces

Treasure your relationships, not your possessions.

—Anthony D'Angelo

Please look at the fourteen steps of the critical connections as they relate to one another. As you think of the names you recorded earlier in chapter 4 of this book, hopefully, you more clearly understand why you have listed those who are truly loyal to you. Although they ascended a sequence of steps that built the relationships you enjoy, it is beneficial to understand the steps of the critical connections.

And of course, the opposite is also true. You recorded the names of individuals who you feel would undermine you, speak evil of you, and be detrimental to your success. It is also extremely important to identify why those relationships have unraveled to determine if they're salvageable.

The critical connections for all relationships

    7.   *Loyalty*
    6.   *Ownership*
    5.   *Commitment*
    4.   *Empowerment*
    3.   *Trust*
    2.   *Respect*
    1.   *Appreciation*

---

    1.   *Rejection*
    2.   *Isolation*
    3.   *Insulation*
    4.   *Hostility*
    5.   *Rejection of Success Symbols*
    6.   *Acceptance of Failure*
    7.   *Crime and Violence*

As you study the chart, keep in mind who you identified as loyal to you. Can you see how the relationship developed? Can you visualize the sequential steps? If so, you have identified the critical connections of the relationship.

Then as you visualize your relationships with those you feel have a serious attitude toward you, you can also identify their place on one of the steps on

Proctor's spiral of futility. The question is, How far down on the chart are they? A person who appears on the spiral of futility does not feel appreciated.

We have seen that it is natural for a person who does not feel appreciated to feel rejected, disrespected, and not wanted by the organization. This is true with husbands and wives with children regarding school and their acceptance by peers or teachers, and it is also true in the workplace and, yes, even in neighborhoods and congregations.

As you reflect on the chart of the fourteen points, give thought to the people you know and where they are on the chart. Consider your own relationships with others in various settings. Can you identify past or a current relationship when you were on a specific step of Proctor's spiral of futility? It may be that you applied for a number of jobs or that you were not promoted. It could simply be an adult softball team where you feel you are not being used, whatever the reason may be. Your relationship might be a group, organization, or congregation of which you are a member, and you feel you are not being used to the extent you are capable. This is often the case in religious congregations when it happens that a person who enjoyed assisting in various roles is no longer used. That person begins to feel rejected—even if it is simply perceived. The effect of unintentional rejection is the same.

Each of the steps in the spiral of futility is naturally a sequential step into deeper hopelessness. When people begin to feel rejected, they automatically begin to distance themselves from the other person or group in an attempt to or diminish the pain of rejection.

I taught a college class in an elementary education department. One evening, when we were discussing Proctor's spiral of futility, a student approached me at the end of class and told me that, for the first time, she understood what had taken place in an event in her life. Her brother had made some mistakes, which hurt the parents to such an extent that he perceived their response to him as rejection. She watched his relationship with their parents spiral downward, and he ended up moving to a different city to separate himself from them.

I firmly believe that it would greatly benefit schools to give serious attention to Dr. Proctor's work. It explains many of the incidences of tragic shootings and other violence. Students do not feel appreciated but rather feel rejected, and they spiral down the steps to crime and violence. Frequently, it begins with those students being victims themselves—until they turn on others who become the tragic victims.

I have been a principal in four different schools and have watched these steps play out time and time again—not only with students but also with employees and parents.

But there is good news: The person in the spiral can often take charge and turn the situation around.

CHAPTER 9

Hope

Every healthy, vibrant, trusting, and loyal relationship provides hope. When a relationship begins to unravel, hope begins to wither away. When anyone begins the spiral of futility, hope seems to be lost.

French General and Emperor, Napolean said "Leaders are hope peddlers." This cannot be done without trust and a true belief in the leader. Does your organization see you as a hope peddler? If hope is absent in those who make up your organization, then there is a serious relationship problem. When leaders have deep and abiding relationships with their followers, then hope is not only present but also alive and well.

If a husband and wife have lost trust in their relationship, then there is a strong possibility that at least one of them is in Proctor's spiral of futility—they have lost the hope their relationship had given them. When hope is gone, rock bottom is near. Theirs becomes a shallow relationship or, at the most, only an endurance challenge. Hope is replaced by an empty, dark place, held together by the commitment of two people who no longer feel appreciated or respected. Their marriage has now become a shallow, empty, and unfulfilling relationship. How sad and such a tragedy for them and all others affected by their marriage. May we as leaders become "hope peddlers" in all relationships.

There is no question that couples, friends, coworkers, and others thrive when the critical connections in relationships are nurtured and vibrant.

Hope also expands creative thinking, and many possibilities become real. A person feels empowered, achieves a sense of ownership, and diligently seeks valuable solutions to help the organization thrive and reach the next level—even closer to the vision.

When a hopeless person is on the spiral and he no longer desires to help the organization that is rejecting him. He will only do the minimum and is part of the problem rather than the solution. This is indeed a very serious reality, costly to the organization.

All relationships take work. Something must be given to help relationships reach their potential. Why not put the necessary commitment into a relationship to derive the best from it? In the next chapter, we will consider how to improve a relationship. This is true whether the person is on Proctor's spiral of futility or ascending on the critical connections chart a healthy relationship.

CHAPTER 10

Strategies to Turn Around a Relationship

A great relationship is about two things. First appreciating the similarities, and second, respecting the differences.

—Anonymous

It would be wonderful if all relationships could be repaired, but sadly, that is not the case. Many people are familiar with Stephen Covey's "emotional bank account." He makes the point that we should not intentionally make withdrawals in relationships because, already, we do too much of it unintentionally, and if we are not careful, we can bankrupt a relationship.

So what can be done when a relationship begins to unravel and a person spirals down the critical connections and enters Proctor's spiral of futility?

The first step in the critical connection's template is *appreciation*. As we considered in an earlier chapter, when a person does not feel appreciated by another person, they descend quickly to *rejection*. Feeling appreciated and feeling rejected are the opposite sides of the coin.

Armed with knowledge of this principle, a leader who intentionally seeks to appreciate the other person has the potential to move the relationship in a corrective direction. It becomes possible to achieve healing for this individual who can move toward a corrective relationship—a healing that is vital to their well-being and their contribution to the organization or family. A statement of appreciation is processed in the mind, but it affects the heart. It thaws out the heart and gives value to the individual.

We might say, "Appreciation serves to open one's window of receptivity." All of us have communication windows. When a person feels rejected, they close the window of their heart and mind. Very little of what is said can get through. Appreciation then unlocks the window and begins to open it to a greater degree of receptivity. The more we respect and trust the person and feel that they accept us, the more apt we are to open the window of receptivity. To a greater degree, less filtering of what is said begins to take place, and the heart begins to thaw out.

Appreciation can be delivered simply by a statement directly to the person. It might be a card or a note stating appreciation. It could take numerous statements and repeated actions of appreciation to begin to move the person off the spiral of futility.

You probably have noticed that people place cards of kindness, thoughtfulness, or simple appreciation on their desks or work areas. Why do they keep these? Why do they place them where they can see them rather than file or toss them? We all desire affirmation. Affirmation is a statement that validates what we want to believe about ourselves.

When talking to ourselves, we constantly look for reasons to validate our beliefs. When another person states it in any form of communication—acceptance, validation, or confirmation—then appreciation takes place. Appreciation is the true foundation of healthy relationships.

Very often, I was contacted by an assistant principal whose relationship with the principal—had spiraled into Proctor's futility. As we talked, I first sought to identify where on the spiral he was positioned. Once that could be determined, we then discussed how he got there. Next we would consider specific strategies for expressing sincere appreciation to his boss. This is not an easy matter, especially once a person has experienced hurt, pain, and rejection. To return to the relationship with a strategy of appreciation is certainly not easy. Truly, not in every situation can we see the relationship turn around. However, it was accomplished and, many times surprisingly, did not take long.

I have had principals follow the appreciation strategy with teachers, and they've reported back to me that the person who was most distant from them had become their closest associate. I have also worked with people in various departments who were close to being fired and have watched them turn the relationships around.

The information I am providing I had originally developed for a training. I conducted variations of the training to school and district administrators and faculties around the country. I have presented numerous other training courses including Time Management for Administrators, Working through Conflict, How to Develop a Vibrant Culture, and Hiring Strategies Involving Ideology and Skillsets. The most requested courses have been The Critical Connections for Success in Every Relationship and Inspirational Leadership which also addresses relationships. The following are some of the comments I received at the conclusion of these two trainings.

"I wish I had this type of training in grad school."

"This training has inspired me and provided methodology on how to inspire my staff."

"I will go back to school with a better attitude and work to become a better leader."

"I now understand how important it is to capture the heart."

"I want to improve relations with the teachers who feel rejected."

"I wish all of the teachers could attend this training."

"I wish current senior administrators in the district went through this training."

I would often hear back, months later, from a principal telling me the employee or student who had been the greatest thorn had become their greatest ally. It was the implementation of the things learned in the trainings, that was the difference maker.

CHAPTER 11

The Family

Having a place to go is home. Having someone to love is a family. Having both is a blessing.

—Donna Hedges

I hope by now you have identified someone whose relationship is worth saving and have decided to work to turn it around.

How about your family? Is there a *parent* whose words have been harsh, expectations seem to have been disappointments, and the relationship is strained? By taking the first step and making yourself vulnerable, you can very well turn the relationship into one you strongly desire. Be the difference maker, offer hope and reopen communication, work through sincere appreciation, and help the person feel valued and affirmed. This may require an inspection to find gratitude in areas that have been overshadowed by pain. Focus on what to be thankful for and express gratitude rather than what annoys you. This is not to neglect the shortcomings, but rather, this is to help both parties find the good that has been overlooked.

How about *children*? It is so easy to allow words to fly; once stated, they can never be retrieved. The relationship suffers. It may have become a surface relationship where words are not even spoken. What if the relationship can be turned around and become vibrant, compassionate, and uplifting? Why not be the healer rather than the hurter, the sunshine rather than the storm cloud? Peace and joy provide a harmonious spirit and rewarding relationships. From these relationships emanate an energy of well-being in families.

How about *spouses*? The divorce rate is so high in America. Even if the paperwork for a divorce is never filed, many couples become merely tolerated roommates. All we have to do is to observe the married couples around us and see the ones who express mutual appreciation and respect. These behaviors nurture love. Appreciation is what happened initially in the relationship and can once again begin to soften the heart and the hurt to recover the relationship. In many damaged relationships, trust must be rebuilt. It takes time, but the effort is a sign the person cares and evidence that he or she wants to make a positive change.

Obviously, the family reaches a greater number of individuals. Where can a rebuilding take place? What can you do to help remove the person from the spiral of futility? If you are on it, what can you do to take the initiative to open the communication and seek to change the relationship?

CHAPTER 12

The Workplace

The workplace is more than a physical location with a name on the front of a building. It may be made up of only a handful of people or it may be a mini city. It can be made up of individuals who see it as a temporary fit for the moment, simply a paycheck or an escape from life's challenges. Some see it as the entry level to a career, while others see it as finally entering their desired career path.

When a new employee walks through the door, some may be limited just to entry level skill, and others bring amazing skills. During their time on the job, there will be family health challenges, the disappointments of life and finances that will weigh heavily upon them, broken relationships, marriages, etc. They bring life weighing heavily on their hearts and minds to the workplace, which can interfere with their productivity. The critical connections within their own families sometime are fragile and weigh heavily upon them.

In addition to the challenges and needs of their physical family, they now become part of a work family.

They are placed in teams and work groups they have not chosen and are hoping for an enjoyable journey. Again, the critical connections for success in relationships are at risk.

We do not have to look very far in a workplace to see relationships affecting others and hurting the organization. Productivity suffers and rejection is apparent. Inevitably, the hostility spreads like a dreaded disease, taking its toll on those who have to be around it.

I have seen situations where employees are pushed to take sides in a warring relationship, the workplace becomes toxic, and people begin to sabotage others.

Many readers who have been in the workforce have experienced a friendly unity, synergy, productivity, and trust put into a very precarious balance.

It is imperative that those who lead will not turn their backs on these situations, but, instead be proactive, not forgetting their greatest resource is the employees.

There are those who may have a title implying they are in a supervisory role as a director, manager, etc. If they have anyone reporting to them, then they have leadership responsibilities. This implies an obligation to everyone they oversee. They cannot place their responsibility on automatic pilot and assume the best. It is up to the leaders to nurture a culture with a supportive, positive can-do energy that flows through the organization—a place where the workers, the greatest company resource, feel the leader is in their corner, compassionate, caring and supporting them through thick and thin. The leader casts a vision, sets expectations, oversees procedures and policies and seeks for each person to be all they can be.

As a person reflects on his or her career, there should be a leader who sought to make a fond and special memory of what a workplace should be. The critical connections for success in all relationships will help the leader take the organization to the top.

CHAPTER 13

Leadership

The greatest leader is not necessarily the one who does the greatest things. He is the one who gets the people to do the greatest things.

—Ronald Reagan

Leadership will make or break an organization. Leadership is influence. It will lift an organization up or it can take it down. Those being led can experience the breathtaking mountain top or the pit of despair. Leadership has everything to do with relationships. The greater number of employees who buy into the appointed leader, the greater the synergy and the sooner the vision can be realized. Since the employees are the greatest resource of the leader, it stands to reason that the leader must give serious thought to the unity development of the employees. The leader is the culture leader. Every conversation and action by the leader influence the culture, pro or con. The competence and character of the leader are under constant scrutiny. A leader should work to have every employee desire their leadership.

I have observed appointed leaders the day after their appointment push new initiatives or seek to build a legacy. Since the employees are the most important organizational asset, it would behoove the leader to make it a priority of truly knowing the employees. Getting to know their strengths, weaknesses, ambitions, contributions, potential, and family will reap the greatest of dividends. Where are they as an organization? What are the strengths and the weaknesses of each team or work group? Where are the personnel gaps that need to be addressed? The antenna of the leader is always measuring the critical connections between the employees and seeking to develop them. It is important for the leader to constantly measure his or her development of critical connections with each employee. This should never be a blind spot for the leader.

There are times a person is appointed as the new leader when the organization is close to death. Drastic steps are certainly necessary to bring about change, but it is never an excuse to violate an employee's dignity. When this is done, respect is violated, and rejection is nearby.

There are many worthwhile books on leadership. Probably many of us have our favorite authors on this important topic. All of us can identify leaders who have been our positive role models.

THE CRITICAL CONNECTIONS FOR SUCCESS IN EVERY RELATIONSHIP

When you think that Jesus described himself as a shepherd, the leader of the human flock, we see that he built trust, and worked what we call the critical connections. He never showed favoritism and saw the potential in everyone. His compassion was on display daily. Jesus led by example. He certainly had serious conversations with those who needed to make change. Jesus never compromised his purpose and mission even in the face of life-threatening persecution and sacrifice. He was a hope peddler even through the worst of times.

We are two thousand years later, and his leadership has not wavered. May we be spiritual leaders and focus on walking his footsteps. Jesus modeled the critical connections daily, and we can learn to do the same.

What does our heavenly Father want or desire? A relationship with each one of us. He initiated the repair by extending the sacrifice of his Son. Many of Paul's letters begin with the phrase "grace and peace." As leaders we should learn from our Father and take the first step to reconcile relationships. There will be no peace without the olive branch of grace. This is a lesson every leader can apply. Life without God is hopeless, and life with God is the endless hope. As leaders, may those we are responsible for be filled with hope.

Leadership is a critical advantage for every organization. Whether it is the family, a small business with a few employees, a large corporation, a school, a large congregation with hundreds of members, or a professional sports team, leadership is the difference maker.

For this reason, it would seem imperative for all leaders to approach each employee with the desire to help that person reach the highest point in the critical connections for relationship success. The positive benefit affects each employee's daily level of engagement and the number of days of work the person will be present. High absenteeism is extremely costly. It would seem to follow that every leader should greatly desire to understand how to connect well with each employee.

It is imperative for all leaders to approach each employee with the desire to help every person reach the highest point in the critical connections for relationship success.

It is my hope you will find the study and constant application of the critical connections for relationship success a lifelong tool you will use regularly.

Leaders in every organization, large or small, will benefit by recognizing, referencing, and using these principles every day. Teachers, parents, leaders in companies, congregations, work groups, committees, and teams will benefit by studying the critical connections for success in every relationship.

You can begin by putting into practice the element of appreciation as the cornerstone for building relationships around you.

ABOUT THE AUTHOR

K. Lynn Wade has been an educator, trainer, and consultant. He has conducted training across the country. Mr. Wade has been a highly requested keynote speaker and trainer in the area of education and has an extensive background in relationship building, effective classroom management, and school culture. He was in charge of leadership training for the eighth-largest school district in America. He taught Classroom Management, a college course, for 14 years. Mr. Wade was requested by the local university to conduct very specialized training for school administrators and teachers to turn around their greatest relationship challenges with students and employees. Because of the great success rate, he was asked to continue with it for a number of years. He was hired by a state organization to mentor principals in challenging schools. Mr. Wade was also appointed by the state of Florida to serve on the Education Practices Commission.

He has received various accolades, including the Principal of the Year three times and Boss of the Year.

He was a public school teacher, curriculum specialist, and principal in elementary and secondary schools, and he was asked to be in charge of leadership training. Upon retiring, he was asked to take over a private school that was close to closing and led it from a small, needy institution to a thriving K-12 school of excellence with double the number of employees and students. It is truly one of the success stories in education. It thrives because of a united faculty, an amazing school-wide synergy within the culture, and an unparalleled work ethic with a can-do spirit by the employees.